GUIDE TO PLANNING THE FIRM RETREAT

by Marc Rosenberg, CPA

Guide to Planning the Firm Retreat

by Marc Rosenberg, CPA

Copyright 2010
The Rosenberg Associates LTD
1000 Skokie Boulevard, Suite 555
Wilmette, IL 60091

TABLE OF CONTENTS

INTRODUCTION

Management retreats are one of the best ways to accomplish the wonderful things that the so-called management gurus tell us our firms should be doing:

- Communicating
- Planning
- Thinking
- Empowering
- Focusing on objectives
- Problem solving
- Shifting our paradigms
- Doing first things first
- Being proactive
- Changing with the times

...all designed to achieve <u>success</u> in our organizations, whether success is defined by profits, growth, survival, happiness, challenge or all of the above.

This Guide is intended as an aid to CPA firms in planning and conducting a management retreat.

Although this Guide focuses on CPA firms, the ideas, approaches and forms included in this Guide are applicable to <u>all</u> organizations.

We hope you find this Guide useful. If you have any questions about anything contained in the monograph, please give Marc Rosenberg a call. He'll be glad to help you in any way he can to make your retreat a successful one.

WHAT IS A RETREAT? WHY HAVE ONE?

Retreats are critically important to a firm's success. A retreat provides an opportunity for key people to meet off premises to plan for the future, devise strategies, form goals and address problem areas. Another objective of a retreat is less tangible than those above, but equally as important: To enhance the quality of the relationships among co-workers and improve communications between them. Firms that regularly hold retreats are usually the most successful firms as well. In fact, these firms frequently point to retreats as the place where many of their successful strategies originated.

It is important to distinguish between partner meetings and retreats. Partner meetings are more operational in nature, usually dedicated to day-to-day, routine, short-term issues or to solving an immediate crisis. These meetings are often difficult to schedule, difficult to start on time and frequently interrupted.

Retreats are different. Retreats are a time for contemplating, communicating, thinking, planning, and building a spirit of teamwork. Although these objectives can certainly be pursued while in your office, they are easier to focus on if the retreat is held off premises, free from the distractions of phone calls, e-mail, clients, questions from staff, the mail and countless other interruptions.

There are **two kinds of retreats**, both worthwhile, but one is clearly better than the other:

- One kind of retreat is convened to focus on certain topics or issues and is successful at conducting fruitful, meaningful discussions on those topics. Participants feel good about the retreat after it is over. However, the retreat leads to no action taken. Everything is business as usual when participants return to the office. But at least the participants have had a chance to get to know each other better, speak their mind and perhaps walk away with different thoughts and ideas—"in their minds" if not on paper.

- The other kind of retreat, which is the better one, has all the characteristics described above, <u>plus</u> it leads to taking action when everyone returns to the office. Later in this Guide, we will describe how to make sure you convene this type of retreat.

Years ago, I discussed the concept of a retreat with the managing partner of one of my client firms. This firm had been in business for 30 years and never had a retreat. When I asked the managing partner why, he responded that the word *retreat* always meant to him "pulling back" or retreating as in battle. He had never retreated from anything in his life and didn't intend to start by conducting a retreat. I explained to him that while some retreats are seen as opportunities to "get away from it all," the intention of a retreat, and of this Guide, is to focus on how to proactively address the most pressing issues facing the firm.

WHAT DO FIRMS TYPICALLY DISCUSS AT RETREATS?

Most firms spend their time at retreats planning for the future, forming goals and addressing pressing issues and problem areas. The problem areas aren't day-to-day issues such as purchasing a new copy machine or revising the policy on sick days. The problem areas are more strategic: morale issues, recruiting problems, profitability, etc.

Here are some specific examples:

- Are you happy with the direction the firm is headed in? Do you have a direction? Does your firm have a formal, written strategic plan?

- Are you satisfied with profitability?

- Is your firm growing at a proper rate? Is your firm active enough in practice development? Do you need a marketing plan?

- Is your firm's partner compensation system performance-based? Is it fair? Does it motivate the partners to do what the firm needs them to do?

- Where do you stand on succession planning? Do you have enough partner-potential people coming up that will provide your partners with an eventual exit strategy?

- Do you have programs in place to DEVELOP your staff into future leaders?

- Do you have sensible plans in place to structure new partner buy-ins and buying out existing partners? Many firms these days are taking a close look at these plans and finding that they are ineffective and archaic.

- Is your firm's management structure effective?

- How effective are your partners and managers in supervising staff in a way that enables you to retain them and help them grow? Firms are increasingly turning to upward evaluations by the staff to help them gauge this effectiveness.

- Does your firm have partner accountability? What needs to be done?

- Should you be looking for merger and/or lateral hire candidates?

- How do you evaluate your staff? What should you be doing to help them develop?

- How is morale at your firm? How can it be improved?

- Are you satisfied with productivity, both of partners and non-partners?

- Do you have effective billing and collection procedures? Are they working?

On the next page, you will find a checklist of topics that firms may wish to review before finalizing a retreat agenda. And remember, this list is by no means all-inclusive.

A good way to decide what topics to include in the agenda is to have the participants complete a confidential retreat questionnaire. A sample is toward the end of this monograph. The completed questionnaires must be sent to someone outside the partner group so that the intimidation factor is eliminated. No one should be able to find out how other participants "voted."

CHECKLIST OF RETREAT AGENDA TOPICS

General Area	Specific Agenda Topic
Management	Strategic Planning: Where do we want to be in 5 years? Goal setting The 25 "Best Practices" of the best firms: How does your firm rate? Role of Managing Partner and/or Firm Administrator Structure of the firm's organization Trends in the industry
Partner Issues	Partner compensation Partner retirement/buyout How to bring in new partners (the buy-in, ownership pct., etc.) Partner accountability Partner evaluation Does the partner agreement need to be modified or updated? Partner conflict and communication Clarify partner roles and expectations
Succession Planning	Succession plan, including transition Partner retirement/buyout Leadership development Introducing the concept of non-equity partners
Mergers & Acquisitions	Upward , sideways and downward mergers
Marketing	Are you growing at a satisfactory pace? Developing a marketing plan Developing niches and special skills Practice development, including training Should we have a marketing director? Do we need to hire a marketing consulting firm?
Operations	Practice Management Review by a consultant Profitability – satisfaction with Benchmarking with Rosenberg MAP Survey Productivity of partners and staff IT needs: are we staying current? Do you have effective billing and collection procedures?

General Area	Specific Agenda Topic
Staff	How to make the firm a great place for staff to work
	Leadership development and training
	Performance appraisal
	Recruiting
	Review of results of an upward evaluation of ptrs & mgrs by the staff
	Review of results of a staff attitude survey
	Mentoring of staff

LENGTH AND FREQUENCY OF RETREATS

<u>Length</u>

Retreats range from one to two days. I have facilitated hundreds of retreats over a period of 20 years, 90% are for one and a half or two days. In deciding the length of a retreat, several factors need to be considered:

1. **Timing.** Resist the temptation to convene the retreat beyond a 9:00-5:30 or 8:00-5:30 work schedule. Even though you may work many more hours than this back at the office, a retreat is different. "Older" adults are not used to sitting in a classroom all day, and many find it quite draining. Participants should be able to spend every minute of the retreat refreshed, sharp, and engaged. So in planning your retreat, don't count on more than 7.5 or 8 meeting hours per day. Be sure to provide for an hour for lunch and two 15 minute breaks.

2. **Objectives.** What are your objectives? What needs to be covered? These are the first questions that need to be answered. If you select 4 or 5 topics, and want to spend the proper amount of time on each, you will probably need closer to two days than one.

3. **Recreation.** Do you want to build in golf or other recreation time? If so, this will make it almost impossible to limit the retreat to one day, and two days could be a challenge.

4. **Session format.** Do you want to build in alternative formats such as educational sessions, motivational speakers or break-out groups? These worthwhile pursuits are time consuming and will require a two day retreat.

5. **Time away from the office.** If your firm has an unusually strong work ethic, and partners will start becoming anxious and edgy being away from the office for too long, you may be better off with a one day retreat. Partners need to focus 100% on the retreat for it to be effective. If they can't keep their minds off of the work they are missing, then you may be better off keeping the retreat short. Another alternative is to convene part, or all, of the retreat on a weekend.

6. **Number of retreats per year.** Some firms convene more than one retreat a year. In this case, two one-day retreats will probably be sufficient.

Frequency

Most firms that have retreats hold them on an annual basis. Firms that convene two retreats per year do so to address various events in their cycle. For instance, CPA firms often convene a retreat just after tax season to critique the season and take a look at the rest of the year. They may also convene a retreat in the fall as more of a planning session.

RETREAT FORMATS: ALTERNATIVES

There are a number of formats you can choose from. Many retreats combine more than one format.

1. **Potpourri Retreat**. This is by far the most common type of retreat. Firms identify a finite number of topics and generally devote 1-4 hours to each topic, depending upon the nature of the topic.

2. **Planning Retreat**. The focus is on development of a strategic plan, a marketing plan, or both. For larger and/or complex organizations to fully address strategic planning, virtually the whole retreat needs to be dedicated to this topic, usually a day and a half to two days. Smaller firms need at least one full day.

3. **Theme-Oriented Retreat.** Most, if not all, of the retreat is devoted to one area such as marketing, development of a partnership agreement, etc. Or, the firm could address several issues, all within the context of one central theme such as service quality or communications.

4. **General Firm Review.** A high level review of all areas of the firm. Essentially, participants conduct their own practice management review. At this kind of a retreat, firms might review their profitability, management structure, compensation and retirement agreements, staff, systems, etc.

5. **First-Ever Retreat**. Although firms convening a retreat for the first time can select any of the alternatives on this page, many firms find it effective to begin their first retreat by addressing some very basic issues:

   - How do we see the firm?
   - What do we expect from each other?
   - What are the firm's greatest strengths and biggest problems?
   - Deal with certain issues for the first time, such as how income is allocated, how the firm markets, what roles each partner should play in the firm, and the need for a managing partner.

WHO SHOULD PARTICIPATE?

There is a natural (and justifiable) tendency to limit participants to the firm's key people. For CPA firms, this usually includes the partners plus key people such as the COO, firm administrator, marketing director and HR director. This way, sensitive and confidential issues are more easily discussed. Also, keeping the group small lends itself to better group participation and hence, more fruitful discussions.

On the other hand, there are benefits to involving others in the firm beyond the key people. If the objectives include empowering the staff, leadership development, making staff feel part of the process, educating them on firm issues or generally making sure that the partners get the staff's perspective on certain issues, then it may be appropriate to invite some or all of the staff.

A big factor in whom to invite will be the agenda topics. If the agenda consists of issues such as partner compensation, partner retirement, analysis of profitability and partner accountability, then it obviously is not appropriate for non-partners to attend. But if topics such as strategic planning, staff issues, marketing and systems/processes dominate the agenda, then it makes sense to invite managers and perhaps supervisors.

Many firms struggle over the issue of including the COO/firm administrator in the retreat. If the firm administrator is to perform at the high level that you should expect, then it's inconceivable that you would consider *not* inviting this person to attend. The COO/firm administrator should be privy to *everything* that goes on in the firm.

A final issue to address is the overall size of the group. At larger firms, including partners, managers and key admin personnel could swell the total number of attendees to 30 or more people. At this size, it's very difficult to get a high level of group participation. In fact, it has been my experience that when the group gets beyond 15 or so, group participation starts to diminish. So, the size of the retreat group is an important consideration in determining who to invite.

When the group gets too big, you need to build in provision for *breakout groups*. With breakout groups, the leader kicks off the issue by making some introductory remarks and then assigns discussion questions to the breakout groups. These groups can all work on the same questions or may each work on a different subject. To maximize the benefits of this approach, all of the break out groups should share the results of their deliberations with the entire assemblage. This approach makes it easier for more people to participate in group discussions.

GROUND RULES FOR PARTICIPANTS

The success of any retreat depends upon active participation by the vast majority of the participants. I cannot emphasize this enough. It has been my experience that the following will <u>severely retard</u> the willingness and ability of the participants to speak up if any of the following are present:

1. Participants see the meeting as being primarily for the benefit of the one who leads it.

2. Participants are intimidated by the way the leader conducts the sessions.

3. Participants who dominate discussions, using up a greatly disproportionate percentage of the "air time" of the group.

4. Participants are intimidated because one or two partners, usually "powerful" partners, are always negative, always telling people "that will never work" or "we tried that years ago and it failed miserably." All participants should be advised: "If you keep on being negative or insisting that ideas won't work, then suggest a better way or shut up."

Although a good facilitator can help minimize the damage by these people, peer pressure is an equally effective tactic. If you see any of the personality types above, speak up yourself and don't allow them to ruin <u>your</u> retreat.

Here are some simple ground rules that I give to my clients at the beginning of a retreat:

1. Every participant should view his/her presence proactively. Think of this obligation in these terms: "The only reason you are here is because you promised to contribute."

2. If you keep ideas to yourself, you are denying the others an opportunity to hear your ideas.

3. There is no such thing as a "wrong comment." Don't be afraid to blurt out something that comes to mind, even if you can't think of a way to say it eloquently.

4. Comments should be constructive. This isn't group therapy. No one should feel attacked.

> If two people have the same opinion, one is unnecessary. It's not going to do me any good at all to communicate with someone else who sees the same thing. I want to communicate with you because you see it differently. I value that difference.
>
> **Dr. Stephen Covey, *7 Habits of Highly Effective People***

5. Distribute handouts so that participants don't have to take notes during the retreat and can concentrate on *what* is being discussed, *when* it is being said. **But participants must be told in very clear terms not to leaf forward in the handouts and to stay on the page being discussed.** The group needs everyone's undivided attention every minute of the retreat.

LOCATION

ONE OF THE BIGGEST MYTHS about retreats is that they need to be held at some luxurious resort, out of town, with overnight stays and spouses invited.

I facilitate about 10-20 retreats a year, and nearly all of them are held at a local hotel conference room, with no overnight stays and without spouses. And these retreats work out just fine! The key is to get away from the office and all the distractions.

Firms that desire to convene their retreat out of town at a resort are certainly welcome to do so. It may represent a nice "perq" that they feel entitled to (and, presumably, can afford). But from the standpoint of getting the most out of a retreat, these extravagances are not necessary.

If you choose to convene your retreat at an out of town location, there are a number of logistical issues that need to be attended to:

- Plan far in advance.

- Try to visit the facility to make sure it suits your needs. Conference facilities are notorious for "over-selling" themselves, describing a cramped, pedestrian work area in a way that sounds like a spacious, state-of-the-art facility.

- The facility should be able to meet all of your equipment needs.

- The facility should be able to accommodate your lunch needs in a speedy fashion. You need to avoid two-hour lunches—it makes for a long afternoon.

See also the "Logistics" section later in this Guide.

TIMING

Select dates for the retreat as far in advance as possible to minimize conflicts with participants' work and vacation schedules. At least 6 months, and preferably 9-12 months of advance notice is suggested. But once the dates are selected, it should be understood by all participants that nothing is allowed to supersede the retreat. This is the one time of the year that client needs and staff needs *always* play second fiddle to *firm* needs.

When considering dates for the retreat, keep in mind the following as potential conflicts:

1. Other firm events.

2. Your firm's busy season or other busy cycles.

3. Major holidays and vacation periods, including religious holidays.

4. Major trade shows and other outside obligations.

5. Critical periods during your firm's typical month. For example, if the first week of each month is the time for getting the billing out and preparing firm financial statements, then it may make sense to avoid the first week of a month in scheduling the retreat.

You may also want to consider the time of the year vs. the subject matter covered at the retreat. For example, putting together a marketing plan for a CPA firm at a November retreat may not make sense, because the tax season will, unfortunately, impede implementation. Analyzing profitability at a May retreat may not make sense because it's too late after the close of the previous year and too early to analyze the current year's results.

Generally speaking, the earlier in the year the retreat is held, the better because invariably goals and plans will be developed at the retreat. With the retreat out of the way early, the firm has the remainder of the year to implement the plans and work toward the goals.

Some firms are uncomfortable scheduling a retreat during the week due to work pressures. In this case, you may want to convene the retreat over a weekend. Some firms compromise with a Friday-Saturday retreat. All of this depends upon the culture of your firm.

Caution: Most people work very hard during the week and look forward to their weekends off. Don't schedule the retreat over a weekend if this will cause resentment among the participants. Attendees at a retreat need to be energized and feel glad that they are there. Don't meet on the weekends if most participants will go through the meeting wishing they didn't have to be there.

In my 20+ years of facilitating retreats, less than 1% were scheduled on a weekend day.

RETREAT FACILITATORS AND SPEAKERS

<u>Every Retreat Needs a Leader</u>

Someone needs to be the leader of the retreat. This doesn't need to be the person who organizes the logistics of the retreat. In this context, I'm referring to the person who runs the sessions, keeps everyone on task, gets participation from attendees, changes topics, monitors the time schedule for breaks, lunch, etc.

The person who leads the retreat should function as a **facilitator**, not as a boss. A facilitator is someone who makes it *easy* and *convenient* for the *participants* to communicate with one another and address the issues raised. A good facilitator doesn't "manage" the retreat, arbitrate disputes, or engage in too much lecturing.

Instead, a good facilitator:

- Gets each topic started.

- Tosses out questions that need to be discussed.

- Achieves a balance of keeping the retreat on schedule while trying not to cut off fruitful discussion.

- Tries to get participation from everyone, including those who tend to be quiet.

- Tones down those who tend to dominate.

The acid-test of a good facilitator is this: Was the group able to continuously engage in animated, productive, enjoyable discussions, with frequent interchange between most or all participants? Did the group stay on task and conclude each topic with action plans for implementing recommendations?

Participants should do *at least* 80% of the talking to the facilitator's 20% or *less*.

One of the biggest mistakes firms make with retreats is appointing one of their own members to run or facilitate the retreat. And the biggest mistake of all is letting the CEO facilitate the retreat, because:

1. The intimidation factor is too great. If the boss is running the meeting, people are naturally going to be reluctant to speak openly and honestly. People who don't speak up at regular firm meetings won't speak up at the retreat. People who tend to dominate regular firm meetings will dominate the retreat.

2. The boss may find it difficult to resist the temptation to lecture his/her troops. To many executives, letting their key people discuss an issue and reach a conclusion is a sign of weakness. They see themselves as decision-makers and are uncomfortable letting a group make decisions.

3. If the boss is the facilitator, then he/she cannot be a participant. This is the one time of the year when the boss can be "one of the guys."

Outside Facilitators

An organization cannot understand itself. Often times, people within the organization mistakenly feel that, because they know what is happening and why, they are the ones that should resolve the problems. People within an organization may know what they are doing, but they will not by themselves learn a better way. Their best efforts and hard work only dig deeper the pit that they are working in. Their best efforts and hard work do not provide an outside view of the organization. This is why a consultant, particularly one with expertise in your industry, can have a profound impact on an organization.

W. Edward Deming

Engaging an outside facilitator for the retreat will enable you to achieve results that you cannot get alone. The outsider brings a "fresh set of eyes" to the firm. The outsider sees your firm in ways you cannot. He/she asks questions that would never occur to you.

Criteria for selecting a retreat facilitator. The best facilitators have ALL of the following:

1. Vast experience consulting to CPA firms. Your firm needs to benefit from the experiences of the consultant. Your firm needs to learn about the best practices that the consultant has observed over many years, working with many firms.

2. Vast experience in facilitating retreats.

3. Consulting experience in the topics on the agenda. If half your agenda is marketing, hire a consultant with lots of experience working with firms in marketing. If a big topic is partner compensation, don't hire a consultant who has never worked with firms in this area.

4. Avoid "big-ego" consultants who love hearing themselves talk, dominate group discussions, tend to lecture instead of facilitate and intimidate most participants.

5. Hire a facilitator who will err on the side of "telling it like it is" in terms of how he/she sees your firm. But make sure the consultant doesn't do this in an arrogant or condescending way.

6. Some "consultants" are really speakers, not facilitators. These people spend most of their time speaking at conferences, training and writing books. You need someone who has been in the trenches with other firms and understands how the partners think.

7. The facilitator should want to be proactive in putting together an agenda, even if your firm knows what they want to address.

8. Ask the facilitator what he/she does to prepare for the retreat. It should be obvious that your facilitator plans on extensive preparation for your retreat. You don't want a "cookie-cutter" approach from your facilitator. The last thing you want is a facilitator who spends little or no time getting to know your firm and preparing for the retreat and starts off by kicking his/her feet up on the conference table and simply saying, "What do you want to talk about?"

9. A good facilitator distributes handouts to the participants. This triples the participants' comprehension rate and enables them to <u>listen</u> to the discussion instead of taking copious notes.

10. You shouldn't have to ask your facilitator to write a report summarizing the retreat and including action items. The facilitator should *insist* on it because he/she wants to make sure you have a game plan for implementation. The facilitator knows that if he/she leaves it to the firm to prepare the retreat summary, it either won't get done or will be done so poorly as to render it useless.

11. A good facilitator will include in his/her report a list of action items or a "to do" list. An example of such a list appears on page 22.

12. A good facilitator understands that the probability of the client successfully implementing retreat goals without his/her help is very low. Your facilitator should be proactive in offering to assist you in the implementation phase and following up with you.

<u>Speakers</u>

In this section, we refer to speakers as someone *other than* the facilitator. Usually, this is a guest speaker, perhaps a "motivation" speaker—an enthusiastic professional able to deliver a message to the participant group. Occasionally, firms opt for an entertainer to lighten the retreat somewhat.

Speakers come from all kinds of sources: professional societies, trade associations, government, sports, entertainment, banks, law firms, educational institutions, etc.

Some firms form a panel of their clients to address the group.

Firms that engage speakers in addition to a facilitator almost always need a minimum of two days at the retreat.

SPECIFIC RETREAT GOALS OR RETREAT "TO DO" LIST

Note that the list below isn't complete until names and dates are placed in every box in the two right-hand columns.

Typically, participants at a retreat have an easy time coming up with a fairly long list of initiatives. Usually, the firm doesn't have the time or resources to accomplish all the goals. Therefore, an important step to take at the retreat is to prioritize the goals.

Think Big. Keep it Simple.

Goal	Responsibility	Deadline
MANAGEMENT		
1. Hire a COO. Salary range $100-150K		
a. Refine/finalize a job description.		
b. Decide how to recruit: ads, internet, search firm, etc. All methods to be used.		
c. Contact AAA and place an ad.		
d. Contact COO that Rosenberg knows.		
e. Talk with lawyers we know.		
f. Agree on focus of the position: HR probably more than other areas.		
2. Need a bookkeeper. Hire the COO first.		
3. Once COO on board, he/she reviews the entire admin staff for having the right people in the right spots and their competence.		
4. Begin to convene partner meetings quarterly instead of monthly.		
5. HR, finance/admin and operations committees may not be needed once COO is on board.		
6. Workflow and QC initiatives will probably continue to involve committees.		

Goal	Responsibility	Deadline
STAFF ACTION STEPS		
1. Need to hire more professional staff, mainly experienced people. Devise a game plan to hire what the group of 4 managers decided the firm needs.		
2. Do a staff survey to identify what morale is. You can't be serious about making the firm a great place to work unless you understand what the staff think of the firm and their jobs.		
3. Consider outsourcing to ease the busy season crunch. Don't limit outsourcing to personal tax returns; consider write-up as well.		
4. Give a presentation to the staff, summarizing what happened at the partner retreat; tell them what the firm is going to do.		
5. Mechanize a system for ensuring that each staff person has a half dozen or so engagement review forms in their personnel files each year.		
6. Create core competencies and criteria for advancement for each title/position.		
7. Need to document the firm's workflows.		
8. The firm should identify specific training areas that partners and staff need. Then, put on internal training programs which would include: • Technical • Soft skills • Computer skills		
9. Develop new staff orientation program that is measured in months, not hours.		

Goal	Responsibility	Deadline
STRENGTHEN TAX DEPARTMENT WITH A HIGH LEVEL PERSON WHO CAN BUILD THE TAX REVENUE BASE		
1. We would like to have a partner-level, marketing-oriented tax partner.		
2. Retain a search firm to find a lateral hire.		
3. Passively search for a merger with a small tax firm.		
LEADERSHIP DEVELOPMENT		
1. Identify those who are experienced enough to show whether or not they have potential for partner; talk with them about what it means to be a partner, what partner promotion criteria are, whether or not they *want* to be a partner, etc.		
2. Create written criteria for promotion to partner.		
3. Participate in XYZ leadership development program.		

LOGISTICS

The retreat should be used to motivate the management team and build a spirit of teamwork. Achievement of these objectives can be greatly enhanced by following a few simple rules:

1. Keep the dress and atmosphere informal.

2. Make sure the facility is suitable. If at all possible, visit the facility before-hand to check it out. Make sure the facility can accommodate lunch in an hour and can arrange for your audio-visual needs. And make sure the meeting space will not be exposed to noise in adjacent areas or rooms.

"Real-Life" Horror Story. I once facilitated an out-of-town retreat at a major national hotel in a large Midwestern city. The meeting room literally shared a wall with a railroad tunnel. Freight trains passed through the tunnel every 15 minutes like clockwork, causing us to pause for 2 minutes or so every quarter hour because the noise from the train (which was literally 30 feet from our chairs, separated by one, inadequately insulated hotel wall) was too loud to speak over. At another retreat, the room next door was used by an organ company (the musical kind). The noise from customers and sales personnel playing the organ was extremely disruptive.

3. Make sure that the room is big enough.

"Real-Life" Horror Story. Many firms convene their retreats in the cozy confines of a local club that has historical significance in the town. But beware. These wonderful symbols of American history create problems for retreat-goers. The biggest problem is that they are too small. Other problems: Lack of climate control, or over-powering noise from an archaic heating/ventilating system. Also, these firms try to have lunch in the same room as the retreat sessions. So during the last half-hour before the lunch break, the wait staff starts setting up the room for lunch, clanging on the dishes and silverware. Guess where the attention of the participants is riveted?

4. Make sure that the seating is comfortable and conducive to getting results.

"Real-Life" Horror Story. One client of mine decided to have their retreat at the seaside summer home of one of their partners. It wasn't until everyone arrived that the host-partner sheepishly informed everyone that he had just bought the house and hadn't "completed" furnishing or decorating it. There weren't enough chairs; the chairs that *were* there were old and damaged; there was no provision for a flip chart (an essential at any retreat) and no central place for a facilitator to stand before the group. And there was no heating. Somehow we worked our way through all these problems, but they were needless distractions.

5. Eat meals as a group.

6. For retreats involving overnight stays, keep the group at the retreat facility from start to finish. Don't allow cliques to form.

7. Absolutely no use of handheld electronics should be allowed when meetings are in session. No one should have their PDA on the conference table; they should be in their purses or briefcases. Calls, text messages and other communications can be made during breaks, but everyone must turn off their handhelds before sessions start.

8. Minimize after-dinner working sessions. Retreats are intensive, draining experiences. Keep everyone fresh during the day by letting them play at night.

9. Minimize day-to-day operating issues in the retreat agenda.

10. Provide handouts for sessions. Don't force participants to take copious notes. Handouts make it easy to follow the discussions. If possible, give handouts out only as they pertain to the discussion at hand. Distributing handouts that apply to future sessions invites participants to leaf ahead while discussions take place on the current topic.

11. Appoint someone to take notes and type data written on flip charts. Some firms bring a trusted secretary to do this. This relieves both the facilitator and the participants from having to take copious notes, thereby enabling them to concentrate on the discussions.

SAMPLE RETREAT AGENDA

Day #1	Topic
8:30 – 10:15 am	Strategic Planning
10:15 – 10:30 am	Break
10:30 – 12:00 pm	Strategic Planning – continued
12:00 – 1:00 pm	Lunch
1:00 – 3:15 pm	Strategic Planning – continued
3:15 – 3:30 pm	Break
3:30 – 5:00 pm	Strategic Planning – continued

Day #2	Topic
8:30 – 10:15 am	Firm profitability: • Rosenberg's benchmarking analysis of the firm • How satisfied are we with profitability? • What do we think profitability should be? • What can we do to improve profitability?
10:15 – 10:30 am	Break
10:30 – 12:00 pm	Staff motivation and morale: • Are we satisfied with our staff? • Are we doing the right things to develop staff? • How is morale? How can it be improved?
12:00 – 1:00 pm	Lunch
1:00 – 3:15 pm	Partner compensation: • Are we satisfied with the present system? • What alternatives should we consider? • Should we change our system?
3:15 – 3:30 pm	Break
3:30 – 4:00 pm	Potpourri—The partners want to discuss: • Are we big enough to have a firm administrator? • Should the managing partner get a bonus? • How many billable hours should the staff work? • Should we adopt the executive committee approach? • Miscellaneous
4:00 – 5:00 pm	What is going to make us implement all the ideas from the retreat? What needs to be done about partner accountability?

HOW TO CONVENE A RETREAT THAT LEADS TO ACTION AFTERWARD

1. Announce the retreat well in advance and agree on agenda topics early enough so that participants can give some thought to the topics and perhaps do some preparation.

2. Use a facilitator to run the retreat, preferably an outside consultant. This will keep the retreat on task.

3. Make sure the retreat follows an agenda. A structured meeting will lead to focused discussions, which facilitate the formulation of specific recommendations.

4. At the conclusion of each topic, make sure the group discusses how to address the issue(s). Make sure the recommendations are as specific as possible and assign responsibility for implementing each recommendation with a deadline.

5. At the conclusion of the retreat, prioritize all the "to dos." One final question should be asked of the group: "What will it take to make us *do* this?"

6. Make sure that the results of the retreat are summarized in a written report, preferably from the consultant. A list of "to do" items should be included.

7. Make sure there are incentives for people to carry out the retreat recommendations. "If there are no consequences to failing to carry out an action step, then it is unlikely that the step will get done."

8. Plan to convene regular meetings to review progress on implementing retreat ideas.

9. Before the retreat concludes, agree on a date for a meeting to review progress of retreat ideas.

EXAMPLES OF TANGIBLE RESULTS FROM RETREATS

1. I was able to suggest some services the firm needed to complement their accounting and tax services and to make their marketing efforts more effective.

2. Changes were made to a firm's overall staffing structure—they didn't have the right mix of people.

3. Partners reached a consensus about criteria for promotion of staff to partner.

4. Evaluated alternatives for partner succession and retirement.

5. Partner duties were rearranged to make the partner group as a whole more productive.

6. The firm's billing rate structure was changed.

7. Re-evaluated the way the firm's administration gets done and by whom.

8. The firm's strategic planning activities were jump-started.

9. The duties of the managing partner were clarified.

10. The firm devised techniques for getting more partner accountability.

11. Some of the partners of a firm had made certain suggestions to the managing partner that had "fallen on deaf ears" for years. When I made the same suggestions, the MP was all ears.

12. A firm had been struggling with how to approach a senior partner about retirement. The other partners couldn't figure out a way to get the senior partner to talk about his plans without offending him. I got the subject on the table in a non-threatening way that led to a plan for succession.

PLANNING A CPA FIRM RETREAT PARTICIPANT'S QUESTIONNAIRE

Your name: _____

(All surveys will be kept strictly confidential. No remarks will be attributed to author by name.)

In order to plan the Retreat and maximize its effectiveness, your input is needed. Please complete the following and return it, in a sealed envelope, to _____by _____.

1.   In terms of the following, what results would you like to see? Exclude the impact of inflation in the numbers below. Strong suggestion: **The Managing Partner should complete the "Prior Year" and "Current Year Projected Actual" columns so that everyone works from the same base.**

	2009 Actual (prior year)	2010 Projected Actual (current year)	2011 (next year)	2015 (five years from current year)
Net Fees (millions)				
Income Per Partner (000)				
Number of Partners				
Total Number of People (FTE)				
Number of Offices				

2. What do you think the two or three highest priorities of the firm should be in the next year?

a._____

b._____

c._____

3. What additional markets should the firm consider for specialization over the next few years?

a._____

b._____

c._____

4. NEEDED IMPROVEMENTS. Check off the items below that come closest to describing your major complaints about the firm. Check at least five items but no more than ten.

Too much emphasis on traditional CPA services and not enough on consulting, specialization and other services	
Insufficient attention to firm management	
Too much emphasis on profitability and productivity	
Not enough emphasis on profitability and productivity	
Too many unproductive partners	
Partner compensation system not fair	
Firm has no direction; no formal planning or goal setting	
Not enough emphasis and activity on growth marketing and practice development	
Ineffective staff retention, development and motivation	
Not enough partner accountability	
Ineffective billing, low realization and/or weak collections	
Doing too much work for clients who shouldn't be clients anymore	
Inadequate professional staff; talent is weak; not enough people at the right levels; lots of turnover	
Inadequate or non-existent succession planning; not enough of our staff have partner potential	
Behind in office technology	
Not enough meaningful partner communication and collegiality	
Ineffective performance feedback to staff	
Ineffective performance feedback to partners	
Outdated or non-existent partner agreement and/or buyout agreement	

5. How can the firm improve its profitability?

a._____

b._____

c._____

6. Rank the following issues that you think should <u>definitely</u> be on the retreat agenda. Assign a rank of 1 to the issue you *most* want on the agenda, a 2 to the second most important, and so on, until you get to 16, which you should assign to the issue you *least* want on the agenda. **BE SURE TO RANK ALL ITEMS!**

		Rank
1	Strategic planning. Where is the firm going? What kind of a firm do we want to be? What is our vision for the future? *Execution* of the plan, not just creating the plan itself.	
2	Partner goal setting	
3	Trends in the CPA profession and how our firm should react to them	
4	Profitability	
5	Partner compensation	
6	Succession planning, partner retirement, and buy-out plan	
7	Mergers with other CPA firms: upward, downward or sideways	
8	How to bring in new partners: buy-in, ownership, compensation	
9	Partner accountability. We have difficulty holding partners accountable for their role and performance in the firm.	
10	Management structure issues: How the firm is managed, roles of managing partner, firm administrator, executive committee, marketing director, department heads and other key people. What management structure should the firm have?	
11	The role of a partner in our firm—let's clarify what is expected of each partner. What do we *owe* each other?	
12	Staff retention, development, motivation, morale, training, recruiting, mentoring	
13	Leadership development; developing staff into leaders and partners	

		Rank
14	Marketing; bringing in business; formalized marketing practices	
15	Specialization; niche marketing; what services should the firm be providing?	
16	The firm's use of technology	

7.   Are there any other questions or topics you feel should be discussed at the Retreat?

a._____

b._____

c._____

d._____

e._____

RETREAT EVALUATION FORM

Rate the following items regarding this retreat.

	Excellent		Average		Poor
INSTRUCTOR Knowledge	5	4	3	2	1
Presentation skills	5	4	3	2	1
PROGRAM Suitability of topics	5	4	3	2	1
Length of retreat	5	4	3	2	1
Quality of handouts	5	4	3	2	1
FACILITIES Location was convenient	5	4	3	2	1
Quality of food and service	5	4	3	2	1
Quality of room & facilities	5	4	3	2	1
OVERALL RETREAT RATING	5	4	3	2	1

What did you particularly like about the retreat?

Suggestions for improving future retreats:

Suggestions for future topics:

NOTES

MONOGRAPHS BY MARC ROSENBERG

How to Bring In New Partners

Succession planning has hit CPA firms with a vengeance. As Baby Boomer partners approach retirement age, they naturally are focusing on who can take their place and eventually write their retirement checks. This monograph answers the questions *What are Best Practices in bringing in new partners? How is the buy-in structured? How does all this work?* Chapter titles include:

- What is a partner these days?

- Should we have non-equity partners?

- How do firms develop staff into partner?

- What does one get for the buy-in?

- When are they ready?

- How do new partners get compensated?

- What should their buy-in be?

- 22 main provisions of a partner buyout plan

- What should their ownership percentage be?

- How should voting work?

- How does capital get determined?

- What about non-solicitation agreements?

TO PURCHASE A COPY, GO TO WWW.ROSENBERGASSOC.COM

How to Negotiate a CPA Firm Merger

Thousands of firms are seeking the only exit strategy available to them – merge into another firm. And most firms over $5M have a voracious appetite to merge in smaller firms. But most partners have never negotiated a merger before. Marc Rosenberg has consulted with firms on mergers for over 20 years. This monograph answers the questions *How do you get started? What can one do before the merger to make sure it's successful? What actually needs to be negotiated?* Topics include:

- The steps in the process

- How to assess the cultural fit

- Keys to a successful merger

- 34 critical questions to ask

- What data should you review?

- Nuances and idiosyncrasies

- Questions the "smaller" firm must ask

- Deal-breakers and non-negotiables

- Questions the "larger" firm must ask

- Key systems that must be agreed to

How to Operate a Compensation Committee

CPA firms are increasingly realizing that the old compensation formulas no longer work, that performance "intangibles" need to be recognized, and that their compensation system needs to be performance-based. This is leading to the adoption of compensation committees by more firms across the United States. This monograph answers the questions *What are Compensation Committees? How do they work? Why have they become so popular?*

- Characteristics of a good system

- Structuring partner compensation

- The link to strategic planning

- Data reviewed by the CC

- The role of partner evaluations

- The role of the firm's Core Values

- Partner goal setting

- Make-up of the committee

- Examples of partner roles

- Performance criteria for partners

- Should the system be open or closed?

- Decisions that the CC needs to make

- Compensation Committee Timetable

TO PURCHASE A COPY, GO TO WWW.ROSENBERGASSOC.COM

What *Really* Makes CPA Firms Profitable

This monograph summarizes dozens of high-impact techniques to maximize firm profitability. Based on Marc Rosenberg's experiences with over 600 CPA firms across the country, this monograph focuses on the most effective techniques and practices. Chapter titles include:

- The Essence of CPA Firm Profitability

- Accountability and Acting Like a Partner

- CPA Firm Benchmarking

- Marketing and the Bottom Line

- Strong Management and Leadership: The Most Reliable Path to Profitability

- Other Ways to Improve Profitability

- 25 Best Practices that Move Firms From Good to Great

- What Doesn't Seem to Be Important to Firm Profitability

- Partner Relations: Happy Partners are Productive Partners

- 40 Great Ways to Improve CPA Firm Profitability

This monograph includes benchmarks from the Rosenberg MAP Survey to rate your firm's profitability.

Guide to Planning the Firm Retreat

The complete guide for planning a successful management retreat. Marc has facilitated 10-15 retreats a year for over 20 years. This monograph walks you through his proprietary process of planning, selecting agenda topics & running the meeting itself, all geared to enable the firm to take action on retreat ideas. Topics include:

- What is a retreat? Why have one?

- What firms typically discuss at a retreat?

- Alternative formats

- Potential agenda topics

- Who should attend; who to invite

- Ground rules for participants

- Location, timing & logistics

- Retreat facilitators and speakers

- Sample retreat agenda

- Examples of tangible results from retreats

- Suggestions for ensuring implementation of ideas.

- Retreat evaluation form

TO PURCHASE A COPY, GO TO WWW.ROSENBERGASSOC.COM

Effective Partner Relations and Communication

Jointly written by Marc Rosenberg and Dr. Ellen Rosenberg, an experienced clinical psychologist with more than 20 years of experience in private practice. They have worked together on CPA firm projects involving partner relations issues, and their experiences are chronicled in this monograph. Topics include:

- A look into the causes of difficulties among partners

- What groundwork should be laid in the beginning of partner relationships

- Partner collegiality vs. accountability: why we can have both

- Communication: What it means, why it's important and how to be good at it

- Picking your partner right to begin with

- Why conflict is good and how to resolve conflict

- When it is best for partners to stay together and when it is best to part

- What partners should talk to each other about

- How to have effective partner meetings

- Partner relations issues common to men

- Health and psychological issues

- Partner relations issues common to women

TO PURCHASE A COPY, GO TO WWW.ROSENBERGASSOC.COM

Made in the USA
Charleston, SC
28 June 2012